A Long-Stemmed Rose

A collection of poems by Mississippi Poetry Society's 2013 Poet of the Year

Patricia Butkovich

Heartfelt thanks to Mississippi Poetry Society for the honor of being named 2013 Poet of the Year and to all South Branch members, especially Brenda Finnegan, who never stopped believing and offering encouragement.

Acknowledgements are due to the following publications in which some of the poems first appeared:

Mississippi Poetry Society Journals and Anthologies

The Magnolia Quarterly

2011 Golden Words-Senior Poet Series, Volume 18

Photographs by Patricia Butkovich

Dedication

For Dave

all my love forever

Table of Contents

Preface

"Use what talent you possess; for the woods would be very silent if no birds sang there except those that sang best."

Henry VanDyke

Life's Like Climbing a Long Stemmed Rose

I'm a caterpillar:
a blond, fuzzy, roly-poly,
creeping up a long-stemmed rose.
I see only the long, green path,
but I cherish a dream of the rose.
I know this stem
with its prickly thorns
is not an eternal home.
I belong in fragrance,
in velvety softness,
in repose— I don't know,
but I'm certain it's there,
as real as the leaf I munch,
and the rain that falls.
The sun that warms.

When nature dictates,
I obey,
sleeping in my silk cocoon—
believing without fear,
dreaming sunrise colors,
endless nourishing nectar,
effortless flight.

April

Cozy months of winter spent
in fleecy, comfy sweats,
passively reclining to view
the latest prime-time fare—
suddenly it's warm,
sunny, and humid.
Azaleas shout, dogwoods confirm
that shorts-and-sandals season's here.
Time to reveal lumpy thighs of inactivity,
sun-starved calves and unkempt toes.

Yes, the glaring spotlight of April
always springs upon me, unawares.
"April is the cruelest month."

Crumbs

CRR...ACK!
was the sound that made heads turn
as I walked my class to the art room today.
It was Jimmy Robbins, that big kid in seventh grade.
He caught the ball, Coach pitched, perfectly with the bat
and sent it screaming down the third-base line.
Dwayne Johnson made a valiant lunge
and got green skid marks all over his gym shirt.
That ball was still smarting from Jimmy's
mighty whack,
as it went speeding into foul territory
skimmed over the row of ligustrum bushes,
then—a dull, sickening, final

CRRRR...UNCH!

A silence settled down around Coach and those kids,
as heavy as that sappy, sweet scent of the ligustrum.
You see, the flight of the ball had ended
in a big crunchy bed of windshield crumbs,
on the front seat of Coach's black Chevy Tahoe.

Death

It floated into her house unnoticed
and stayed on for years
like wispy smoke
curling into corners,
lurking in shadows,
and stealing things.
First it was a large, round portion
of her vision from the center
of one eye. She adapted and continued
baking her prize chocolate cakes,
starching ruffled kitchen curtains,
and keeping all the floors gleaming.

It tried to steal her breast,
so the doctors cut it off.
Bits of her memory and bones
disappeared next.
She grew shorter
and no longer wrote letters.
Still, she kept a perfect home
and continued working for her church.

When she could no longer see the road,
her son took over driving her to town.
She couldn't attend church services,
so church friends came to visit her.
She hired help to cook, wash and clean,
adding a walker to steady failing balance.

Then one spring, the wren house her son made
and hung in the old oak near the kitchen window
was for her, just a blur—so he watched, told her
they'd returned, and cracked the window
to let their song float in with the breeze.
She regularly saw the great grandchildren,
ever loving and advising them.

Bolder now, Death started taking her dignity,
stealing just a little every day
until she was almost like a newborn babe.
One day as I sat and held her hand,
she said, "Everything is peachy.
It's all just perfect."
With calm and peace upon her face
and a hint of a smile,
her unfocused eyes saw things I could not see.
I knew
the angels were caring for her now
and death, with nothing left
to steal, would seep out
through the cracks
in search of someone else
with much good health.

Bird Nest

There's a bird nest
in the bush;
I gaze upon it every day
in the yard
by my office window pane.
Carefully woven,
probably lovingly—if birds can love;
I like to think they can—
by parents in some year past
to hold and shelter
fragile babes
growing in the eggs
their mother laid…
The incubation vigil
followed by the feeding frenzy,
that first fledgling leap
from the cozy home.

The birds are gone now.
The nest
sits empty and silent,
ignored by all,
and slowly wastes away.

Pruning

"It's for your own good,"
I assured the bushes as
I trimmed back leggy,
irregular branches
that had no direction.
"You'll grow much fuller
and be more attractive
after your post-bloom pruning."

I pray to God that I recall my
own advice when He
sees fit to prune
an overblown ego,
and bring that wild
new growth of conceit
down to size, then feeds
me a heaping scoop of humility.

Thank you, Lord, for pruning
my sinful, unshapely ways.
Guide my growth, that it is well
rounded and full in Your light.

Cell Sonnet

The millions live obeying national law.
The few rebel from God and man to make
The millions live in fear, and they withdraw
From social life and even trips forsake.

Extremists filled with hatred toward mankind
Outwardly seem to be like you and me.
Inside the heart and mind with evil grind.
They do great harm to all, don't you agree?

The same as rebel cancer cells that trick
Good cells and live with them and multiply
So quietly, then seek to make one sick,
Are seen when it's too late to modify.

Dear God, I pray, pluck out the evil few
For You can see intent that is untrue.

Poetry Club

Caressing each word with her tongue,
tenderly lifting it from her journal,
she sends it off into the air
in search of an open ear,
a warm mind,
and a friendly heart.
The words include a bit of soul
woven into the wooded scene
(the still, murky-green pond
and the dragonfly lovers
she once drank into her mind).

Through the art of poetry
I can relive the scene
that so moved the writer,
recall scenes of my own,
discuss common feelings,
and feel a spark of friendship.

Southern Gardens

a haiku series

Showy magnolia
as delectable as that
famous Southern charm

Azaleas ablaze
bounteous feast for the eyes
honeybees' banquet

Heady gardenia
petals so easily bruised
like blooms of first love

Bougainvillea vine
trailing magenta blossoms
queen of the garden

In the Spring of 1947

A package arrived today
wrapped in brown grocery-bag paper
carefully cut to fit and turned with the plain side out—
white cotton string knotted at each crossing
addressed in large letters with a blue ballpoint pen.

In all of my eight years plus seven months
Grandma's never sent a package!
I love the cards with a dollar tucked inside.
Mama says she shouldn't send her money;
there's barely enough for her and Grandpa.

Snip the string and tear off the paper:
"To my darling little Granddaughter—
We're so proud that you've started piano!
This will help you know how long to practice.
With all our love, Grandma and Grandpa."

When I lifted the lid of that box,
there, in the newspaper padding,
was a brand-new ladies watch
in fourteen-carat gold!

Porch Swing

A creamy white (as I recall)
clean and perfect, this old swing
when carried home from Hanby's Hardware
in an age of long ago.

White paint coats piled up like building blocks
until we chose a fresh, clean, forest green—
just the spot to enjoy the breeze,
peruse the news, and inhale the morn.
Mr. Wren would sometimes perch
and whistle to his wife, nesting in the oak,
but only if old Tom wasn't napping on the seat.
Those glossy green slats
soaked in peanut-butter fingerprints
attended teddy-bear tea parties
were privy to revelations
whispered in a full moon's glow.

Like the rings on a tree trunk, the green layers grew
as the breezes of time eased across the porch.
Then we painted it burgundy red and rich
with a seat-pad print of staunch, bold stripes
inviting friends to gather
linger with a cooling drink and some easy conversation.

The swing is silver now;
throw pillows angle in the corners.
Evening closes in around us
as we gently glide
thighs touching, hearts intertwined
humming a song from yesterday
to the rhythm of the squeaking chains.

Music Sonnet

How privileged I seem to be each day
As I attend to all my routine chores;
My husband, the musician's, work is play,
He practices for hours on end with doors
Open so the melodies fill the air.
I soar *On Eagle's Wings* to mop and dust
Wind's Beneath My Wings while meals I prepare,
Pinch dead blooms and water the plants to *Just
a Closer Walk with Thee*, then on to fold clothes.
Honey-drenched jazz chords, soulful melodies,
Arpeggios hover like bright rainbows
Pleasing the senses, reminding of woes.

Timeless pleasures link past to present;
Artist's mood melts with composer's intent.

Since the Day We Met

I love the way you say my name.
It's been that way since the day we met.
It's the special way it rolls off your tongue.

The day I first met your family,
Self-doubt melted as you said my name.
It's been that way since the day we met.

Wheeled through the hospital hallway,
My face was as white as the sheets.
You shouted my name, and I heard.

Company party, I knew very few.
I marveled that they knew me.
You must have been saying my name.

When I quit and say, "That's good enough,"
You say my name, but I hear, "That isn't your best."
It's been that way since the day we met.

A touch in the dark
A warm embrace
I love the way you whisper my name.
It's been that way since the day we met.

Happy Homes Have

honeyed hugs heaped high
humor—hinge to harmony
hemmed in honesty

Sweet, Clear Notes

The music in my life is you.
I have all kinds of sweet, clear notes,
but how they fit, I've not a clue.
The music in my life is you.
The beat I cannot hear is true.
With just discord I cannot gloat;
the music in my life is you.
I have all kinds of sweet, clear notes.

Pain

It takes some hurt to make health feel good
Be thankful when your heart beats strong
We take it for granted more than we should
It takes some hurt to make health feel good
I'd spare you the pain if only I could
But the Lord, in His wisdom, knows that is wrong
It takes some hurt to make health feel good
Be thankful when your heart beats strong.

A Red, Red, Rose
(with Apologies to Robert Burns)

My love's not like a red, red rose
A b-flat minor fifth is he
Warm as the southern wind
Complex as the waves at sea.

You're tall, rugged, and handsome
Lyrical is your embrace
You're like a cool jazz tune
That's played with style and grace.

And fare you well, my only love,
Though we be at our summer home
Or in the warm and sunny south
I never far from you will roam.

I loved you yesterday
But love you more today
And I will love you still, my dear
Though the ice caps melt away

The tropics turn to deserts
And wildlife goes extinct.
You're part of me, my dear
Our lives forever linked.

Fresh Start

The sun is just yawning, but not yet up.
The morning air's so easy to breathe—
dew on the grass sparkles like snow
as we slip out the back door,
my husband and I, our clubs in tow.

The crack of the driver contacting
the ball seems flagrant in the silent air.
We trudge past sleeping condos and houses,
leaving a temporary trail
on the dew-laden fairway.

Two herons arrive at the lake
eager to greet any fish.
A frog angrily chides us
for his being disturbed,
then leaps into the water to hide.

Putts ski across the white green
(No need to keep score
'cause we play just a few.)
This stillness will soon fade away
as crew and players start their day.

Journey to the Creek

a gloss

We ran as if to meet the moon
That slowly dawned behind the trees,
The barren boughs without the leaves,
Without the birds, without the breeze.
           "Going for Water" by Robert Frost

We ran as if to meet the moon.
Our veins were filled with lust to live;
a world so new, it beckoned us.
This night, it sparked like fireflies.
Tomorrow, distant, dim, and thus
we ran as if to meet the moon

that slowly dawned behind the trees,
its path, so smooth and wide, at first,
became quite steep and slowed our flight.
We clung to one another then;
the woods were dense, and blocked the light
that slowly dawned behind the trees.

The barren boughs without the leaves
were hovering like preschool moms
and we cared naught for a foe unseen.
At last the moon was high above;
its silvery light could seep between
the barren boughs without the leaves

without the birds, without the breeze.
Then just ahead, the creek we seek;
its moonlit waters seem to glow—
you go across, for it's your time.
The bucket filled, back home I go
without the birds, without the breeze.

Seventh Day

a pirouette

In the morning it's church:
Learn the Ten Commandments
List the beatitudes
Live by the golden rule
Hold fast to instruction

Hold fast to instruction
In the afternoon, too
A light grip on the club
Always keep your head down
Eyes remain on the ball
Remember to yell, *Fore.*

Bust

The artist, a master
The likeness, outstanding
The medium, perfect
The presentation, apt
The critics all have raved,
"That's a beautiful bust."

"That's a beautiful bust."
Said the chief of police,
"Undercover agents
Posed as art-loving guests
And caught the would-be thief
Attempting to steal it."

Night Race

It was perfection
that normally dwells only in dreams;
that late June night, shirt-sleeve comfy,
wind blowing a steady fifteen knots
across the starboard quarter
into the mains'l and towering spinnaker
pushing our racer
to hull speed.

The sunlight reflecting to earth
from the surface of the full moon
cast a shadowy glow on the deck and sails
making flashlights optional, even at the midnight hour.
It was a surreal, timeless, floating world
as the bow cut sharply through the black restless water,
and swished along the polished hull.

The dark night waters that
managed to reach above the hull and spill
across the deck were alive with
shimmering specks of phosphorus.
So hypnotic was the sight,
that I found an appreciative *oh* or *ah*
escaping my lips
repeatedly.

The sea and the boat were like
dancers meshed in harmony
to the beat of music
playing only for their hearing.
The sea, in a dazzling jeweled gown,
flowed gracefully around and over the deck
receded coyly, only to return
more lovely than before.

This euphoric time-capsule faded with the dawn
as other sailboats and the finish line came into view.
Though it happened many years ago,
I've only to close my eyes
and I'm there once more
rushing through the sparkling, moonlit water,
trimming the spinnaker
as we race to Pensacola.

Weather or Not

Rain: blessed by thirsty Midwest ground
but cursed by flooded coastal homes
amounts just right and crops abound
Rain: blessed by thirsty Midwest ground
too late in fields grown dry and browned
these crops just food for rhyming poems
Rain: blessed by thirsty Midwest ground
but cursed by flooded coastal homes

My Rooster Found Another Chick

Other hens no longer know me.
Out of this coop I'd like to flee;
That would be worth most anything...
I'm just a chicken with a broken wing.

Up to the roost at dusk, I cannot fly.
Down on the floor, I must get by.
Not caring what the night will bring,
I'm just a chicken with a broken wing.

I cannot get into the nest
To lay my egg with all the rest;
Can't eat or drink or do a thing;
I'm just a chicken with a broken wing.

When rooster crows to bring the dawn
My heart is dark, all hope is gone.
Perhaps the farmer my neck will wring
I'm just a chicken with a broken wing.

As I sit by the fence, waiting to die,
A bird as blue as the sky comes by.
He chirps, "Cloud-white feathers are a fine thing
But you're a chicken with a broken wing."

"Your comb reminds me of the red sunrise
That golden beak is to be prized.
A hen with beauty such as yours should sing
But you're a chicken with a broken wing."

I feel a twinkle in my eyes
I think bluebird is very wise
I stand up, and fluff up, and call,
"Maybe my wing isn't broken at all."

Cat Eyes

Oh to dive into the sea-green ocean of those eyes
that stare so intently into mine
paddle down, down into their depth
through the window to your thoughts
to see me from your point of view
as you regally query mine when
I murmur gooey compliments, then
stroke your chin and throat.
Do the cares of your day flow
down the drain with mine
as we cuddle on the couch?

Oh, to feel the contented pleasure
that your smile and purr exude;
to feel my body melt into
the back ridge of the couch,
the corners of an empty shoebox,
or the lavatory bowl.
All places that you find so comfy
for an afternoon of napping.

And to s-t-r-e-t-c-h the feline way,
feel the pleasure that your mew proclaims.
Like a ball of clay, you seem to have no bones
as your front faces one way
while your back goes the other.
Then you stand and become a children's slide
or practice a bow, should you ever greet the queen.
You could teach the yoga masters a thing or two,
my lovely, furry friend.

Cat Chatting

How does one converse with a cat
Who doesn't know—that she's a cat?
Lounges on the couch, as if it's a throne,
Has never munched a mouse's bone,
Thinks stalking bugs is just bizarre;
Prefers to ride on the dash of the car.

Atop the neighbor's fence she'll stroll
Extolling her charms to the guard dog below;
A sailor on a sea of dusky lime
Followed us in for a swim, *one* time.
How does one chat with a cat
Who doesn't know—that she's a cat?

It's best to have a lap, for her to nap.
Let her in when she gives that screen door a rap;
Just behind the whiskers, scratch her cheeks,
Get up when it's breakfast that she seeks.
That's how I speak to a cat
Who doesn't know—that she's a cat.

Sam and I

It was a love affair that began and ended in the street.
While on my daily walk, we met. A highbrow,
handsome and well-groomed, he moved on sure, quick feet,
greeting me, a stranger, with a royally refined meow.
He slept like a vagabond in the cockpit
of our trailered sailboat. We had to meet
in shadows. Hubby said, "No more pets!"
Jealous indoor tom agreed
by hissing hatefully through sun-porch screens.
For me, it was unfettered love at first sight.
Although affectionate, *his* heart I had to glean.
I knew it was, finally for him, all right
the day he offered me a red bird,
ruffled and blinking with shock, softly subdued
between sharp, deadly teeth. My gifts to him were
collars that disappeared in a day or two.
He endured two days locked in the workshop as status quo,
while I called his name and combed the woods in vain.
When Hubby finally saw him, sitting in the window,
he relented and our love affair continued in plain
sight. Reading the Sunday paper, I think Sam would concur,
was a favorite pastime. His demur head nudges were
an invitation for my fingers to romp in his fur.
Though always patrician, a cuddle would start his musical purr.
His unquenchable passion for genteel living
ended one late spring eve, when in a heartbeat,
two headlights speeding through the dark were unforgiving.
It was a love affair that began and ended in the street.

Walking the Dog

I'm towed down the drive by a furry brown speedboat, her nails scratching into the concrete, trying to gain just a little more momentum. A few black-eyed Susans bob and nod a pleasant good morning. Irritating goldenrod just stares toward the sky. He wouldn't speak if he could. We head east this morning. My eye catches the flash of a cigarette lighter, and I squint to see into the shadows of the open garage. It's Nonie; she waves. Saw her husband last week when I stopped in with a loaf of nut bread. All that's left of him now is a frail, bony frame with a translucent skin covering. No sign of Tom. The eaves on his house seem to droop, and the windows have lost their bright sparkle. The pots that stand by the entrance have sprouted a few weeds, and the drive lays waiting for the wind to sweep pine straw and dead leaves away. Abruptly, the neighborhood sideshow begins. A chorus of five yapping voices announce the show is about to start. Little black heads just clearing the fence start popping up here and there. Their legs must have springs, for they're not very big, and that fence is six feet high. The show continues till the audience has passed by the corner. When silence returns to our ears, Dee Dee settles down, stops pulling, and trots calmly along beside me. The fifties-style ranch is where Greg lives. It's a rental. He and his family moved in last year. We'd see him then, most every day out alone on his bike. A skinny kid, he'd wobble along with us always talking, talking, talking. Saw him in his yard once this year. He's grown at least a foot, and his voice has dropped an octave or so. My arm's jerked again as Dee Dee jumps up at a swallowtail butterfly that flitted too close. I see that the cypress vines have started blooming. Those little, bright red trumpets against the vivid greenery might look good on a Christmas card. Tomorrow I'll bring the camera.

Hands

a pirouette

> *Lazy hands make for poverty*
> *but diligent hands bring wealth.*
> Proverbs 10: 4 (NIV)

Papa and Mama saved
Bought land rich and fertile
Planted crops, raised cattle,
Sheep, hogs, and a garden.
Diligent hands bring wealth.

Diligent hands bring wealth
That God stores in heaven.
They lived the Golden Rule
Folded hands in prayer
Gave their all to the child.

Sam and the Squirrel

Brown eyes fixed on the canna plants
Fur coat soft as a breath of air
Tail curled into a question mark
Munching seeds, appears unaware.

Blue eyes peer between the canna
Brown-tipped ears stand at attention
A statue, except for tail tip
Then a blur of furry motion.

A chattering rebuke comes out
from high in the tree someplace.
Sam's amid the sunflower seeds,
and the question mark is on his face.

Coming Home from Summer Vacation

Cicada chorus sings in stereo
Leggy flowers outgrow their borders
Plump garden spider at home by the door
Heavy, humid, Southern air clings to sticky skin
Magnolia cones wear a welcoming blush
Crepe myrtle torches nearly extinguished
Perky pampas grass plumes speak with a nod
Gray dust and stale air occupy the house
Like old friends, each room smiles a welcome.

Polka Dots

Bold-golden polka dots
Dancing with the grasses
Glowing and laughing
In September's sun
Plump black eyes
Beckon me
To sway and smile
In the happy breeze.

My Dance Card's Full

When viewed from afar, she's gorgeous:
Her face a swirl of fluffy white clouds
Gliding so gracefully round one dark eye
Beneath this guise of innocence—
A Jezebel's demonic strength.

No one waits for the party to start!
Her dance floor is slowly cleared
As big, lumbering, paint-chipped working boats
Beside sleek, polished pleasure craft big and small
All decline her attempts to seduce.

This wanton Jezebel dances steadily over the water
Rebellious, intimidating to those in her grasp
One slap of a long watery arm
Snaps lines, rips cleats right out of a deck
Smashing with fury relentless into the seawall unyielding.

All seek to be wallflowers now,
As she swirls around the once-straight pines
Unwilling partners, they twist and turn and bow to the ground
Splintering in the roar of her wild embrace
This harlot'll have her own way as long as her strength holds out.

It's gloomy down here in the closet 'neath the stairs
The hands on my watch seem reluctant to move
As a furious hurricane rages outside.
She could lift off the roof with just one little flick
Of a long, dark, twisting, frenzied finger.
Then it abates, quite suddenly, in the vacuum of her eye
Each cautious step outside is taken as though
She is hiding, watching, ready to start her wild dance again—with
me.
The house has suffered a few scratches and bruises
She has spared some of the trees, but not leaves or limbs.

There on the leeward side of the house
I spy a tiny, gray bird. It's very still and so calm.
It appears unhurt, but doesn't fly from my touch.

Stay put little bird—

for we've seen only half!

Floods

A low formed, clouds gathered,
Pressure dropped, wind picked up,
Water hysterical.
Floods came to our Gulf Coast.

Floods came to our Gulf Coast;
They came from everywhere:
Ready to help clean up.
Big-hearted folks, God sent.

Fall

haiku series

Gulf waters are warm
low pressure in the tropics
hurricane season

Hummers are gorging
beauty berries are purple
nature's calendar

Magnolia cones blush
crepe myrtle spikes gone to seed
markets selling mums

Equinox

Day equals night
Night equals day
Libra is balance
Should not life also be in balance?
Labor and leisure
Income and bills
Sultry summer days wane
As cool, crisp autumn arrives
With gorgeous, golden, harvest moon
A time of celebration
A time for ripening
A time of dying
And we must choose to go on singing,
like the grasshopper—
or, as the ant, prepare for winter and live.

October Dusk

The man in the moon reveals half his face.
Colors of daylight linger in the trees
where some are wearing shawls of golden lace;
bulging cattails defy a dying breeze.

A V of geese lands smoothly on the lake,
joining the flock with loud, raspy greeting;
there's much wing-flapping as they make
room with the others resting and eating.

A fat, red squirrel walks slowly down the oak.
Flicking his tail and warily eyeing
me, finds one last acorn before night's cloak
demands he retire to a nest lying

safely in the branches high overhead.
Another day is forever put to bed.

Symphony of a New Home

First Movement: Allegro

A flute faintly plays a tune
that resonates throughout my mind:
  We need to move,
        to a lake,
                in the woods,
                        secluded from the daily grind.
Soon the strings begin to hum in harmony,
then horns trumpet that they're inclined,
and percussion adds an exclamation point.

Second Movement: Adagio

We explore the harmonics of floor plans
Looking for consonance in each design,
      in arrangement of the furniture,
          in a day-to-day routine,
              in entertaining house guests,
                  the ease to wine and dine.
Cost and budget can't be dissonant.
Plan after plan we decline,
till one strikes a perfect chord.

Third Movement: Scherzo

Sales list and map in hand,
we spend days searching for the site,
    waltzing around the lake
        up and down the hills
           over logs and into ravines
               giving several deer quite a fright.
The lot must play a proper countermelody.
Providing the windows, a view, with good light.
When one strums a dominant chord, an offer is made.

Finale: Allegro

The house will be built in a factory.
Now, it is time for a road trip.
    Models are just what we need,
        to look and to touch,
           to open and to try
               everything from tip to tip.
We march through the endless choices;
shutters, shingles, lights, on and on, even paint chips.
When the cabinet knobs are chosen, it's complete.

Hey There

"Hey, do you remember me?"
flames across my facebook page.
I strive to picture how you must have looked,
when you were six years old.

Did you have long, abundant hair
held in place with a big, bright bow,
colors matching the crisp, cotton dress,
white anklets with lace edging,
and patent leather shoes?
Did your eyes dance with anticipation,
but your hand tightly clutched your mother's
as you carefully settled into the desk
with your name taped in the corner, that first day?

We danced through the nursery rhymes,
sang the alphabet, learned each letter's sound
We read and read and read:
Run, Dick, run.
Run fast, Jane.
See Spot go.
Jump, Sally.
I remember the triumphant smile
as you waved a dog eared paperback, announcing,
"I just read this book; I CAN READ."

The wall of windows opened full,
parents loaned us extra fans,
also sent Kool-Aid and cookies.
We couldn't use the metal slide
till just about October,
but wore a dusty hole
under each and every swing.

We told scary stories for Halloween,
dressed like the Indians and Pilgrims
for a Thanksgiving feast.
I remember the soup mug
with a picture of the Campbell kids,
your Christmas gift to me.
"Inappropriate," said your mother,
but *you* knew that I liked soup for lunch.

We shivered through the winter,
learning how to add and then subtract.
Learned Easter poems, wore rabbit ears
and did the Bunny Hop
for parents packed in every seat.
We made cards for Mother's day;
marked tests required for the records.
Too soon we hugged that one last time;
you boarded the bus and were gone.

Though it seems like yesterday,
that facebook photo tells me
you are much too young to be THAT girl.
Computers would have helped *you* learn to read
in the air-conditioned room of our new school;
where calculators aided math
and Christmas gifts were incorrect.
Could it be that I'm recalling
the day your *mother* started school?

A Candle Lit

A candle lit for peace
A plea that war will cease
The urge to hate released
A heartfelt love increased

For this I light a flame
And let my light proclaim
A lasting peace on earth
Surpassing gold's great worth

Let's light our candles all
A flame no longer small
To show the world full-scale
That peace and love prevail

There'll be no war or pain
When Jesus comes again.
Until we see that day
Hope in our hearts will stay.

The sun,
As each day dawns,
Floods planet earth with light.

Sent to flood every soul with light
...the Son.

Autumn Roadsides

Handfuls of black-eyed Susans
Glitter on November's roadsides
Like shiny golden coins
Spilled from Mother Nature's purse.
Goldenrod brushes pregnant with pollen
Towering above purple ageratum puffs
Monarch butterflies
Sipping nectar
Bees hover, intent on getting their share—
I wonder if the pollen ever
      makes
          them
              sneeze.

Haiku

Melodic jazz tunes
soar in crisp November air
sweet harvest of chords

Thanksgiving Pantoum

Bow your head to pray on Thanksgiving Day
Praise those who've gone before
With foresight, sacrifice, and faith, they
Built the USA to be hope for those who reach its shore.

Praise those who've gone before
Who hunted, fished, cleared, plowed, planted, and
Built the USA to be hope for those who reach its shore.
Give thanks for blistered hands that formed our homeland,

Who hunted, fished, cleared, plowed, planted, and
Though today, turkeys live in freezers and pumpkin in a can,
Give thanks for blistered hands that formed our homeland
And penned the still-strong constitutional plan.

Though today, turkeys live in freezers, and pumpkin in a can
We mustn't let those patriots who gave their lives in war
And penned the still-strong constitutional plan
Ever fade into a past that we ignore;

We mustn't let those patriots who gave their lives in war
With foresight, sacrifice, and faith, they
Can never fade into a past that we ignore:
Bow your head to pray on Thanksgiving Day

Morning Walk

I see justice as tiny wrens attack
and a pesky jay flees

Hear truth in the silent, leafy
canopy of tall, august trees

Smell fragrant peacefulness floating
on sweet clover's lavender sea

Feel God's kindness amid the buffet
of seeds and ripening berries

A daily taste of nature's way
sates the spirit that lives in me.

Angel Sonnet

The headlines read, *Angels Helping Angels,*
Unlike ordinary newspaper fare
Of murders, wars and misdeeds—just angels
Working quietly, without a fanfare.

This angel tree helps children whose parents
Currently are serving time in prison
The children's behavior was not errant,
From this need, the angel tree has risen.

As soon as the paper ran the story
Volunteer angels popped up everywhere
To buy and wrap gifts, not to seek glory
But to give Christmas toys and clothes to wear.

They walk among us, maybe live next door:
It's not just in heaven that angels soar.

Deck the Halls with Christian Love

Christmas star of Bethlehem
That shone upon the crib that night,
Shed your light on us and them;
Melt hatred with your light so white.

Long ago, an angel choir did sing
As the Babe was born to save mankind.
This year may angels to each person bring
the message that He is still here to find.

Shepherds came from nearby hills to see
this infant king so meek and mild
May Christians shepherd others with this plea
To worship down on bended knee,
Mary's holy Christmas child.

December Wedding

An angel in white beaded satin
Floats down the aisle
To her prince;
Eyes sparkling with youth
Face shining with inexperience.
Red Christmas plants
Scarlet-gowned maidens
Raven-suited groomsmen
Mary, Joseph, and the babe
Join the mélange of friends and family,
Beaming approval of this union.

And the two become one…
Words so romantic!
But consider two eggs in a bowl
Touching, but separate
This union must survive
The fork tines, wire whisks
Blenders and sauté pans of life.
In fifty years, will they become
Perfectly blended with savory spices
Peppered with colorful memories,
Hearts melded like creamy cheeses,
Into a happy, golden omelet?
Even the air smiles tonight
On the birthday of our Lord
As a lifelong journey
In matrimony begins.

Shades of Christmas Past

Shades of Christmas past
Sparkle in the mini lights when
Aunts, uncles, and hordes of cousins
In-laws who I barely knew,
Mingled in between
Colorful extended tables laden,
And mounded gifts round tiny tree.
Elders not yet sleeping
Beneath the icy earth.
The youngsters hadn't scattered
Like fluffy dandelion seeds
In gusts of summer winds.

A slippery path carved to the door
Lined-up boots dripped by the door
The bed mounded to the post tops with heavy outerwear
Punch bowl for the children
Stronger drink for grown-ups
Weeks' worth of baking now
Displayed on Christmas plates.
While men rehashed the sports
The women chewed on family news
And children eyed the piles of gifts
Toys and pjs wait for eager little hands
Bottles filled with sweet cologne or lotion,
and, always, chocolate-covered cherries
I didn't even like.

Christmas lights now twinkle
On a tree that has no gifts
Spilling from beneath its branches.
Silence reverberates
Across the spacious floors
Over empty Christmas platters
Into the cold, dark kitchen.
But in each happy, twinkling light, I see
The warming shades of Christmas past.

Mom

a pirouette

One night I chanced to see
Mom fitting Santa's beard
on Dad's round, ruddy face.
I can't forget the sight
that Mom could not recall.

"That Mom could not recall,"
the boy next door once said,
"was the day I had games,
my turn to take the snacks,
and when they gave awards."

Home

Somber, stony clouds
crowded the sky
over the frozen mounds
of freshly loosened earth
that we picked our way around
to reach the icy chairs
huddled together in the tent
the year that Mama went home for Christmas.

A tiny, aging, artificial tree
planted in a dollar-store vase
on a table near her bedside
was the only glimmer of the season
in a home turned empty and cold
by an army of invincible cancer cells,
the year that Mama went home for Christmas.

That night, the lights on the tree
twinkled and triggered a spark
in a heart left empty and numb
as I pictured her radiant reunion with Daddy,
seeing the baby they lost on day one.
Her eternal mansion is surely filled
with all the selfless love, joy, and happiness
she gave to those who touched her life
all the years before Mama went home for Christmas.

May the New Year Be

dewdrops
on a morning rose

the warming sun
on a chilly day

a really good haircut

a fresh breeze
to sail on the sound

frosty milk with
freshly baked gingerbread

and a new pair of red shoes
with spiky heels.

Beware, the Giver

Twins were born on a January cold
Only one drew a breath, as the story's told.
In a Mississippi town, where they did dwell.
A gift sent from heaven, or from heaven's fallen angel?

Went to school all week and to church on Sunday
Minded his elders, but with friends he'd horseplay.
Strummed the guitar and sang quite well—
A gift sent from heaven or from heaven's fallen angel?

Just a nail-biting, sandy-haired country boy, soon
To hit the charts with a bluesy, pop tune
The girls did swoon over "Heartbreak Hotel";
A gift sent from heaven or from heaven's fallen angel?

Playful twinkling eyes, jet black hair with some wisps askew
Curl of the lip and a lustful shoulder shake, all that Ed would "shew"
Caddies purchased by the dozen, gifts to friends he did dispel.
Gifts sent from heaven or from heaven's fallen angel?

Pills to sleep, more to wake, in Hollywood, Vegas, Memphis,
Graceland, fam'ly, friends, hoards of fans he couldn't dismiss
First to broadcast by satellite; rock and roll king nonpareil.
Gifts from heaven or from heaven's fallen angel?

At forty-two, his heart stopped beating, they found him on the floor
The angel of this world, the angel of darkness, gave no more:
No happiness, peace, hope or love, he was just an empty shell,
A final, everlasting gift from heaven's fallen angel.

Robin Red-Breast

Movement makes dormant grass alive:
Every tree and bush is in motion
when I go for the paper in the drive
Barely noticed by this army
Seeking sustenance to survive.

The air is crowded with chatter—
Their winter vacation, perhaps—
Discussing where they did scatter
In sunny southern Florida
To gorge themselves and grow fatter.

Maybe the melodic wagging tongues
Are telling where they will summer
Build nests and raise their young
In the mountains, on the plains
Or an urban song that might be sung.

Whatever it may mean, they say,
"Cheerily, Cheer-up."
My spirit smiles, a happy day!
The message that I hear:
"It is spring; hooray!"

Smoke

a pantoum

The gray swirls and curls melt away
Leaving only a smoky smell
And just a speck of ash so gray
I bid my history farewell

Leaving only a smoky smell
Mountain in the attic removed
I bid my history farewell
Overflowing closets are improved

Mountain in the attic removed
I can float into tomorrow
Overflowing closets are improved
No feeling of loss or sorrow

I can float into tomorrow
Without papers from the decades
No feeling of loss or sorrow
My annals in the air pervade

Without papers from the decades
And just a speck of ash so gray
My annals in the air pervade
The gray swirls and curls melt away

Wal-Mart Paved Our Pitcher-Plant Bog

For many years on the edge of town
A lovely grass-filled meadow
In spring took on a yellow glow
As it donned a flowered gown—
Then Wal-Mart paved our pitcher plant bog.

Each yellow lantern blossom
Hung on a candy-cane stem
The petals making a dainty, scalloped hem…
But asphalt's what it's now become
Since Wal-Mart paved our pitcher-plant bog.

The multitudes of gaping pitchers
An attractive lure insects explored;
Little biters we abhor are just what they adored.
But to make the city richer,
Wal-Mart paved our pitcher-plant bog.

Now citronella candles smog the air
And we keep on hand an array of spray
Shopping is convenient, though, twenty-four hours every day.
The yard and garden shop is big there
Since Wal-Mart paved our pitcher-plant bog.

Grief

She'd bend forward (till her flowered dress hem
hid those sturdy black lace-up Oxford shoes
she always wore), push her pink-plastic-framed
glasses to her hairline slightly askew,
and wring a washcloth of grief stored within,
spilling from her eyes, sprinkling the grassy
mound as if it could somehow seep deep in
the earth, through sealed concrete, to encompass
earthly remains. Her baby who, alas,
died much too young, a mere fifty-four, an
inverse order no mother should be asked
to endure. She'd proclaim what a good man
he'd been, ask God for mercy in His plan.

Then she'd straighten herself, washcloth wrung dry,
keeping it deep inside where no one could see
to absorb more grief, an endless supply
that oozed from her heart, and call out to me,
"Come along now, my precious granddaughter.
We must stop for things from the list I brought."

Beads and Moon Pies

A patchwork quilt of people
Casual, costumed, debonair
Jovial, stolid, face paint, sun shades
Packed along the thoroughfare

Music from the four directions
Converges on the ear
Beads, doubloons, and Moon Pies
Fill up the atmosphere.

Mermaids swim in waves of foil
Glittered shrimp boat packed with krewe
Octopi in deep-sea chambers
Pirate's treasure chest to view

King and Queen eye their realm
Aboard a float with gilded throne
Bedazzling satin sequined guise
Champagne toasts to set the tone

Now a single, printed blanket
Of outstretched armed solicitors
Shining toothy faces calling,
"Throw me sumthin', Mister!"

Doubloons and Beads

Her face was a mirror of the burdens she bore
As through the airport I watched her scurry.
She was pleasant enough and answered our queries
But her eyes were dulled with care and worry.

We had to hurry, there was barely time,
To grab a quick lunch of po' boy and gumbo
Then find a place, 'cause it was 'bout to roll—
Still, as we waited, her brow kept a furrow.

The faces in the crowd were happy and eager.
Showing off proudly the wild costumes they wore,
Youngsters danced happily around the adults
Their impatience sprouting from every pore.

It all started in a blur of color and sound
And went on in a flurry unstopping. By and by
I noticed that she was now smiling,
And I think I could see a spark in her eye.

The king and the queen have chosen teal satin
Sewn with thousands of beads and sequins so bright…
The theme is King Neptune with creatures of his realm.
Doubloons and beads are the crowd's delight

Each huge, gaudy float, done in colors of the sea,
Carries masked riders throwing trinkets and beads.
Who cares that they're worthless in dollars and cents?
All arms try to grab more than anyone needs.

When her neck is covered with plastic-bead shine
She's gotten the spirit and what it's about.
Reflexes sharp, she jumps, dips and mimes:
"Happy Mardi Gras Day!" she now calls out.

After Katrina

a pirouette

Mardi Gras floats did roll
amid debris and mold
past white Fema trailers
because in this Deep South
it's steeped in tradition.

It's steeped in tradition
Southerners aren't puny;
spirits can't be drowned by
a record-breaking surge—
the coast will build again!

Toxic Spring

It gushes, it spurts, it pours
millions of gallons, we're told
since the explosion and the fire
they said could never happen.

Oil and water don't mix
so the island of putrid goo grows
nutrition for our engines
poison to the living.

Tankers pump detergents
as toxic as the oil
making the ugly, orangey grunge
hover on the bottom of the Gulf.

Out of sight, out of mind...
for us, the land dwellers.
But what about the shrimp?
Bodies sticky with sludge
as they crawl along the ocean floor
through insalubrious waters
gasping for life...

Bits of Sun

There's a bit of sun under the ground in my yard
When winter's gloom hangs heavy in the air
My spirit, like last year's leaf, brown, sere, hard
Branches of my mind, as redbud, lay bare

Tiny shoots of inspiration peek out
Undaunted by icy wind and gray skies
Spring is coming, my being wants to shout.
Bits of sun burst forth and smile to all—Arise!

Act Two Is Spring

Ol' Sol's march to the south proceeds
Finches flock to the seed-filled socks
Squirrels forage for overlooked seeds
Snapdragons stand in their spiky frocks.

March winds strip limbs of leaves browned
Rosy Camilla blossoms have posed
Then joined the petal rug on the ground
Leggy pansies pull winter's curtain closed.

Red buds peek out from the wings in costume
Wild jasmine vines high in the pine
Send out golden megaphone blooms
Calling Spring, the next act in line.

Plump azalea ladies parade
While Easter dogwoods serenade.

March

a haiku series

Wispy hot pink clouds
floating on a teal blue sky
beautiful sunrise

Wind whisks sere brown leaves
derelicts from season past
boughs cleared for new buds

Bush tips swell with life
migrating sparrows chirping
goldfinch turning gold

Sun peeking through trees
song bird chorus practicing
winter's chill hangs on

Pickup Truck

It's a quarter to twelve.
No need to look at the clock;
I know the time because
I find myself listening,
Straining to hear the familiar sound
Of Daddy's little black pickup truck,
New about ten years ago…
As he shifted into second gear
To climb the steep gravel driveway;
Then the slam of the screen door on the porch
"Dinner ready?" as he breathed in the aroma
Coming from the pot roast on the stove,
Threw his denim cap
Upside down on the floor,
The sweat stained head-band showing,
And walked to the kitchen sink to wash away the field dirt.

The stove is cold today
The air just air to breathe
Mother wanders slowly into the kitchen
Stands by the window and stares
At the tailgate of the truck
Protruding from the garage.

She's been listening too.

Childhood Twice Lived

a gloss

Yes we'll walk with a walk that is measured and slow,
And we'll go where the chalk-white arrows go
For the children, they mark, and the children, they know
The place where the sidewalk ends.
        "Where the Sidewalk Ends" by Shel Silverstein

Oh we race through our youth without thought, without care
Then a family and job pin us down to life's track.
Keep the dream, till we're old. We'll be free to go there.
Yes, we'll walk with a walk that is measured and slow,

Take our time, ease the pace, so we'll know every face
Be at peace, feel content in our skin and our life
We will roam on the highways and paths of each place
And we'll go where the chalk-white arrows go.

To the top of the mountain on winding byways
And we'll play just as long as we please in the sun
By the sea, on the tee, or our deck where we stay,
For the children, they mark, and the children, they know

And it's children we become as years tune the mind
We know God, trust in God. He is all that we need.
Childhood twice lived—that's the way we can find
The place where the sidewalk ends.

www.ingramcontent.com/pod-product-compliance
Lightning Source LLC
Chambersburg PA
CBHW040936110426
42739CB00026B/5